Kids love reading
Choose Your Own Adventure®!

"When I figured out there were maps on the back, I almost exploded!"

Sophia DeSanto, age 9

"I read them because they are interesting, and they have lots of cool titles and words to use."

Laini Ribera, age 9

"There can be at least 28 ENDINGS in it and so many choices. Other books you have to read the whole book in order, well not this one!"

August Backman, age 10

"I like that you can choose. So, if you want to choose something, you can do it."

Colin Lawrence, age 10

"he CYOA books are crazy because ere are so many crazy choices."

Isaiah Sparkes, age 12

P9-DFY-415

TATTOO OF DEATH

BY R. A. MONTGOMERY

ILLUSTRATED BY MARCO CANNELLA

CHOOSECO
WAITSFIELD, VERMONT

Book design: Stacey Boyd, Big Eyedea Visual Design

For information regarding permission, write to:

CHOOSECO

P.O. Box 46, Waitsfield, Vermont 05673
www.cyoa.com

Publisher's Cataloging-In-Publication Data

Names: Montgomery, R. A. | Cannella, Marco, illustrator.
Title: Tattoo of death / by R.A. Montgomery ; illustrated by Marco
Cannella.
Other Titles: Choose your own adventure ; 22.
Description: [Revised edition]. | Waitsfield, Vermont : Chooseco,
[2006] | Originally published: New York : Bantam Books, ©1995.
Choose your own adventure ; 159. | Summary: After befriending two
boys at the martial arts studio you attend, you are made a member
of the Red Flower Gang and become involved in a plot to smuggle
illegal immigrants into the country from China. Do you go along
with their plan or fight?
Identifiers: ISBN 1-933390-22-0 | ISBN 978-1-933390-22-2
Subjects: LCSH: Martial arts--Juvenile fiction. | Illegal aliens--
United States--Juvenile fiction. | Human smuggling--United States-
-Juvenile fiction. | Gangs--Juvenile fiction. | CYAC: Martial
arts--Fiction. | Illegal aliens--United States--Fiction. | Human
smuggling--United States--Fiction. | Gangs--Fiction. | LCGFT:
Action and adventure fiction. | Choose-your-own-stories.
Classification: LCC PZ7.M7684 Ta 2006 | DDC [Fic]--dc23

Published simultaneously in the United States and Canada

Printed in Canada

12 11 10 9 8 7 6 5 4 3

This book is dedicated to the concept of freedom, liberty, and justice to all. Thank you, founders of this democracy.

BEWARE and WARNING!

This book is different from other books.

You and YOU ALONE are in charge of what happens in this story.

There are dangers, choices, adventures, and consequences. YOU must use all of your numerous talents and much of your enormous intelligence. The wrong decision could end in disaster—even death. But, don't despair. At anytime, YOU can go back and make another choice, alter the path of your story, and change its result.

Meeting new friends in martial arts class seemed innocent enough. But the next thing you know, you have a tattoo on your arm and belong to the Red Flowers, a gang involved in smuggling human cargo! You need to escape! But how? These people play for keeps. You had better practice your karate kick, because you are going to have to move fast to beat the most dangerous gang in town.

You can't sleep. You haven't been able to sleep through the night for almost a week. The last threat was so strong, so frightening that you look behind yourself all the time expecting one of them to be there. Now you roll out of bed and sit at your computer, writing down your story.

This dangerous situation all started about five months ago. You joined a *tai chi* group to help build your confidence and develop your athletic skills. *Tai chi* is an ancient Chinese martial art that stresses defense more than attack. You chose this form of martial art over the much more aggressive arts, such as *judo*, *shotokan karate*, and *tae kwon do*. You just don't see yourself as the aggressive type. You don't want to hurt anybody. The thought of breaking boards with your hand is as repellent to you as pulling the wings off butterflies.

But…what you thought was going to be a simple learning experience has become a nightmare.

You remember the first day when you went to *tai chi* practice. There were two Asian-American boys about your own age who said they were beginners. One was named Ben and the other Sprazzle. You should have known from the start that anyone with the name Sprazzle should be a little suspect. But they were nice and friendly.

Turn to the next page.

Ben was a natural at *tai chi*; Sprazzle was a spazz. You did quite well, and you liked the smooth, studied, slow movements that allowed mind and body to coordinate. You imagined people hundreds of years ago doing these exact movements, and you felt a sense of connection with the past.

The *tai chi* master was named Hunang Fanng. He was from mainland China. "See your hands as parachutes," he instructed you that first day. He showed you how to raise your hands slightly above head level, let your wrists go loose, and allow your palms to drift slowly downward. Then he helped you move them into a rounded position, as if your hands and arms were cupping a large ball. It was relaxing and fun.

One day, about four months into class, Hunang disappeared. Someone said he had problems with immigration. But now you question whether the authorities were to blame.

With Hunang gone, Ben and Sprazzle moved in quickly. Looking back, you see it was a setup. They invited you out for a snack. Even though you tried to pay, they wouldn't let you. That's the way it was. Step by step, they built a web of friendship and obligation. After the snack came a free movie; another time they took you out for a full day to Catalina Island with two of their older friends. You treated them to sodas and snacks, but they paid the fare for the ferry ticket and for lunch. *Big-time mistakes,* you think!

Turn to the next page.

4

Your two friends turned out to be recruiters for the Red Flowers, one of the newest Los Angeles gangs. By the time you discovered this, it was too late to back out. You were going to be initiated!

After a day of freebies at the ballpark, Ben and Sprazz led you to a long black limo waiting outside. It was driven by a heavily muscled man in his thirties wearing dark glasses. You soon learned that he was nicknamed the Anaconda, after the South American killer snake.

"Get in, wimps, I don't have all day to babysit," he grunted. He slammed the car into gear and peeled out as though the police were chasing him. Fifteen minutes later, you were blindfolded and led up three flights of stairs. You could smell the briny sea and the overlay of pollution...

Suddenly the blindfold was ripped off!

"Okay, you slimy snail slug, you child of an unborn ox, you worthless dog, are you ready?" Ben asked, his face twisted in an evil grimace.

"Ready?" you replied in a shaky voice.

You noticed the Anaconda lounging against a wall, chewing on a toothpick. Then Ben stalked toward you with a large electric needle.

"We are giving you the name Tulip," Ben barked. "Now you will get the mark of the Red Flowers on your arm."

Go on to the next page.

ZZZZTTTT! ZZZZZTTTTT!

It took a painful fifteen minutes for the red flower design to appear on your flesh. Sprazzle loved seeing you squirm.

"Okay, Tulip, now you're marked. But to be a true member of the Red Flowers you must do what we say. Got it? You will have a final test to prove your loyalty to us." Ben turned to Sprazzle and the Anaconda. "They have all completed such a task. Are you ready?"

"I guess so," you managed to squeak.

"Louder, Tulip," Ben commanded.

"Yes!"

"Yes, what?" Ben asked.

"Yes, I am ready to make a sacrifice to the Red Flowers," you finally replied.

"Good. You will arrange a meeting between your father and our leader, Big Guy, in Japan."

"I can't do that," you replied. Fear had done a cold-water dance down your spine. Your father is a famous attorney who is running for the governorship of California.

"You'd better. We've got the goods on you and your father," Ben answered with a sneer.

Turn to the next page.

6

You weren't sure what Ben meant, and you didn't wait to find out. As Sprazzle led you to a back room, you broke free of his grip and scrambled down the wooden stairs to the street. You thought the Anaconda would chase you, but he didn't.

As you ran you heard Ben's cool voice trail after you. "That's right, Tulip. Run away. But remember you are one of us now. You can never escape."

Go on to the next page.

This all happened about a month ago. Now there is a death command out for you. You have disobeyed the Red Flowers.

You finish typing your story and slip a copy of it into a sealed envelope addressed to your dad's attorney. You want people to know the truth in the event that things go bad, really bad. You enclose a letter to the attorney, a man named Marvelous Marvin Carmichael, asking him not to open the document until you are deceased. You hope he never has to open it, but your instinct says he may be opening it soon. Really soon.

Time to go. You grab the package and set out for the mailbox on the corner nearest your house. You look over your shoulder all the time. This could be the day, the hour, and the instant that you have feared for the last twenty-two days. Since you ran away from your initiation, the Red Flowers have been sending you threatening messages. They said they would kill you if you didn't do what they ordered. They also said they'd blackmail you. Big deal. If you're dead, what good is blackmail?

The coast seems clear. You pick up your pace. The box is within sight. Your heart rate climbing, your pulse pounding, you hear sounds you have never heard before. Your mouth is dry, your palms clammy.

Turn to the next page.

You make it! You open the slot of the mailbox, and the thick envelope lands with a slight thud. As you turn around you expect to feel a knife slip between your ribs, or to hear the muffled report of a silenced gun, or to feel the gagging pain of a garrote around your neck.

But nothing happens. You're alive; you can breathe; you can see the sky; you can even appreciate the smog and the familiar way it clogs your nostrils and burns your lungs.

Maybe, just maybe, you think, *there is a way out.* The problem is this: the Red Flowers is a gang of smugglers. Their main commodity is smuggling people into the United States from China and other Asian countries. The Red Flowers charge a lot of money for the trip. Their poor victims line up like kids at a movie for the privilege of being fleeced of every cent they have ever earned. They are forced to live aboard  some leaky old tramp steamer below decks for three to four weeks with hundreds of others. The food is rotten, the water brackish and scarce, the sanitation almost nonexistent. People die aboard these ships and those who survive get dropped off in small boats a mile or two from shore. Many are captured upon landing or drown trying to swim in. All in all, it's a dirty, dishonest, and despicable business.

Go on to the next page.

Now you're wrapped up in the business, too. The Red Flowers want to use you to influence state officials to help them smuggle people in. As Ben warned, they do have the goods on you. These so-called friends videotaped you when they robbed a store. They handed you the money before you knew what was going on. It's all on tape, and they have it.

To make matters worse, they also have you on video and telephone recordings arranging the pickup of a delivery. What a surprise! What you thought were rope-soled sandals used in *tai chi* practice was actually a package of stolen goods.

In their last threatening message, Ben and Sprazzle told you, "Either you get your dad to do favors for us, or we'll turn the video files over. You won't like that, and he'll like it even less. We can actually prove your father was involved. Don't forget, when you made the telephone call, he sent his driver to pick up the shipment."

You don't see your dad often because your parents are separated. He lives in San Francisco, and you live with your mom, a businesswoman, in Los Angeles. Your dad would definitely help you, but you fear telling him would break his heart and ruin his career. The favors the Red Flowers are asking for add up to your dad doing business with a criminal syndicate. To go along with them would mean an end to his chances of being governor. No, you have to protect him.

Turn to the next page.

10

Your feverish mind has worked out three possibilities: one, submit to their blackmail, but offer to go to Japan to meet with Big Guy in place of your dad; two, go into hiding until you can think of a way to turn the Red Flowers in and not get hurt; three, go to the cops. What a position to be in. *Life isn't supposed to be this way,* you think.

*If you decide to go to Japan,
go on to the next page.*

If you decide to hide, turn to page 26.

*If you decide to go to the cops,
turn to page 53.*

The next time Ben and Sprazz contact you, you agree to meet them and talk. "Listen, I'll work with the Flowers," you say. "But why not send me to Japan? You'll have more control that way than if my father goes."

Ben and Sprazz give you the once-over. They don't really trust anybody. But then, why should they? After all, these two thugs are in the crime business. They're making money on people's lives. Sure, they're not killing them, but they're doing something just as evil. They're importing them illegally, like guns or drugs or money.

"Don't forget, you're tattooed, Tulip!" Sprazz says menacingly. "You're marked for life. You're ours and always will be."

You'd like to see the cops catch old Sprazz and send him away for a really long vacation, but that isn't your problem now. You've got to convince them you are still part of the Flowers. Then and only then can you get to the top, identify the right people in the gang, clue your dad in, and wait for the arrests to follow. It sounds easy, like an afternoon movie where the good guys always win. Trouble is this isn't a TV show; this is real life. The tattoo on your arm proves that.

Turn to the next page.

12

"Hey, I'm cool, I'm with you. I'm not bailing out." You hope they believe you.

"Well, if you're so cool and all, how about proving it?" Ben gives you one of his long stares. It's supposed to melt weaker people's minds and turn them into plain yogurt past the edible date.

"I offered to go to Japan, didn't I?" you reply, acting a little tough.

"Not enough!" Ben says. He is serious. You can see it in his eyes. "Before you go we want you to deliver this package for us. No questions asked. Got it?"

A small, flat, rectangular package wrapped in plain brown paper sealed with duct tape rests on the table. You look at it, and it seems to glow. It could be anything: a letter bomb, drugs, or a ransom note. These guys are bad, real bad. Of course the package doesn't really glow. It's just your overactive imagination.

"Sure. I'll do it," you hear yourself saying. Your mouth is flapping, words are coming out, but inside you are screaming for help.

The package sits on the table beckoning you to pick it up and deliver it.

"Where to, *kemo sabe*?" you ask.

Turn to the next page.

14

"The statehouse. The governor's office. It's kind of a present, wouldn't you say, Sprazz?"

"Yeah, Ben, a present he'll remember," Sprazz says, laughing. "And we got ourselves a real nice messenger."

With your heart in your throat and your hands feeling like broken glass, you take the package and head for the door and the outside world that seems so normal. But you and the package could spell death, disfigurement, or tragedy for a lot of people.

Once you are outside, an idea pops into your brain—*open the package and check it out before you deliver it!* This is a ridiculous thought.

But what is the alternative? Lie about it. Tell Sprazz and Ben you delivered the package and hope they won't find out that you didn't. Or deliver it and hope it doesn't blow up and kill somebody.

The Red Flowers don't like people who waste their time. Act now!

If you decide to open the package, be very careful, and turn to page 16.

If you decide to get rid of it, turn to page 24.

So that's how you become famous. Your testimony against the Red Flowers is all the police needed to round them up, charge them, and try them. They're behind bars now, but in a way, so are you. You're in a witness protection program and living in Hawaii. Your hair is a different color, you wear contact lenses to change the color of your eyes, and you have a new name.

Sometimes you think back on it all and regret that you didn't stay the course and act as a decoy for the police. You could have gotten deep within the Flowers and helped unravel the whole rotten network, right back to Hong Kong, where the poor souls who end up as captives begin their hopeful journey to a new world. You know well the horror of these people who stake their life savings on the promises of smooth-talking criminals who treat them like cattle to fill up their bank accounts. Slavery is as old as the world; how to really stop it still remains the big question.

The End

16

Courage sometimes comes when you least expect it. Against your instinct for survival, you carefully unwrap the package.

First the duct tape. Nothing happens!

Then the first layer of brown paper: corner by careful corner.

Still nothing!

The last layer is red paper similar to the wrapping used on Christmas presents. You pull it off slowly and are startled by what you see.

It's a picture of the current governor accepting money from Big Guy himself. There is a wad of bills in the governor's hands and a grin a mile wide on his face. The picture is signed:

With appreciation for all you do for us.

There is more where this came from.

Your friend in the Flowers, BG.

You wrap it up, and with great sadness you deliver the package, insisting that it be given only to the governor. You feel like a rat. But did the governor really take money from the Flowers? Years ago, when he was a crusading young district attorney, there were ugly rumors that he was on the take. *Maybe it's just catching up with him,* you think. You are eager to go to Japan and find out what's at the bottom of all this. If the Flowers still want you to go.

Turn to page 19.

18

You decide to warn them. Slowly you climb the trellis, gain the roof, slip inside the house, and head carefully back down the steps. Ben and Sprazz are chattering away and listening to a small music speaker turned down really low. They look like a couple of kids at a party, not like two young criminals about to be eaten by a snake named the Anaconda.

Your heart pounding, your ears thrumming, you reach deep inside you where the power, the energy, the calmness reside. You find them. You step down onto the floor, turn to Ben and Sprazz, hold your hands to your mouth, and point outside.

In a whisper you say, "There are thugs outside who are going to kill you. You can either believe me and escape with me, or you're goners."

Ben and Sprazz stare at you in amazement and disbelief.

"What are you, the fairy godmother or something? You're the one who needs to escape. We're going to send you on a nice long trip," Sprazz says in a loud voice.

Ben stops him. "What do you mean?" he asks.

"Look outside!"

Ben follows your eyes and sees the shape of the big car and the chauffeur. The silhouette of a man can be seen in the interior of the sedan.

Turn to page 21.

They do. You passed the test. Ben and Sprazz congratulate you on your return. This gang thing is all about tests and loyalty to a crooked code of ethics. Mess up once and you get punished; mess up a second time and the punishment can be permanent. You didn't mess up, and you are off to Japan.

The idea of the trip is exciting—and frightening. Ben and Sprazz are kids playing in an adult world of bribes, payoffs, and money drenched in blood. The horrible thing is that it reaches all the way up to the offices of lawyers, business leaders, and government officials. Now you are going right into the heart of this evil. Big Guy is as corrupt as they come.

Still, you board the plane. You want to stop this menace to your world. You want to help put an end to modern-day slavery.

Turn to page 23.

"So? We were expecting the Anaconda and Big Guy. Big deal." Ben pauses and looks at you suspiciously. "Why would you warn us anyway?"

"Because, Ben, I'm not like you and Sprazz. Because I give people second chances. Because it is the code of the warrior to be fair and to do what is right."

"Nice speech," Ben says, an angry curl to his lips. "Tie him up, Sprazz."

The door opens almost silently. The Anaconda enters. He's armed and grinning a semi-toothless grin.

"After you tie Tulip up, tie up Ben, and then I tie you up, Sprazz," he says.

Before he can do or say anything more, you dash for the door. You squeeze through but end up smack in the arms of a second thug.

"Always check, always be prepared, always be ready," he mutters. "You acted from impulse without real thought. You lose!"

That night the sharks in the bay—the Great Whites, the hammerheads, and a few blues—eat well. Ben and Sprazz are their dinner. You are their dessert.

The End

You land at Narita International Airport in Tokyo. The trip takes three days, five thousand miles and twelve exhausting hours in the air.

The crowds are the first thing that hit you when you finally get through customs and passport control.

A slight, smiling, well-dressed young woman is waiting at the exit to passport control. She holds up a sign that reads TULIP.

"That's me," you say, going up to her. *Can she really be involved with these creeps?* you ask yourself. *No, she's probably just a messenger and doesn't know anything about them.*

"Please follow me," she says with a smile that seems forced. She leads you to a taxi, and you both get in.

"Meridian Hotel, near the Ginza," she says in English to the driver, who looks like a bank president. He's dressed in a gray three-piece suit and tie and wears white cotton gloves. The cab is a German import; spotlessly clean and smelling like the inside of a fine luggage shop.

Turn to page 31.

24

Getting rid of the package without the Flowers finding out is as likely a happening as a teacher not collecting homework. Your head swims with the frightening possibilities of what Ben and Sprazz will do to you when they discover you have disobeyed orders. Not to mention what Big Guy and his adult hoodlums will do. The thug named Anaconda is feared from Hong Kong to Minneapolis and back. He could make your life—or what's left of it—very unpleasant.

So what do you do with this package? You could chuck it and hope that the gang believes you delivered it. You could say you were mugged and that the package was stolen. Or you could fake an accident with a car. If you pretend to get hit, you can end up in the hospital with amnesia and no package. You'll be relatively safe there, you hope.

*If you fake an automobile accident,
turn to page 30.*

*If you decide to say it was stolen,
turn to page 90.*

*If you decide to just chuck the package and
trust the Red Flowers will believe you delivered
it, turn to page 104.*

You decide to trust Sabaruki. But despite all the careful preparations she makes, Big Guy is one step ahead of her. His brain, assisted by the computer, has evaluated all the information available and developed a list of potential paths that Sabaruki and you might follow.

With the computer's prodding, Big Guy accepts the notion that Sabaruki hates him and wishes him harm. The computer even develops a scenario chillingly close to Sabaruki's plan. Big Guy prepares for her.

You and Sabaruki are captured before you can act. You are taken by private jet to Hong Kong. As the computer is programmed for profit when it does not perceive an imminent threat, you are sent to work in a faraway country rather than killed. So you're alive, and while you're alive there's always hope.

The End

26

The Red Flowers are dangerous, so you decide to go into hiding. This will give you time to decide how best to proceed. You remember an important principle of *tai chi*: instead of confronting the oncoming rush of an adversary with equal force, you position yourself to use your opponent's energy to cause him or her to run right by. Or you return the energy in such a way as to unbalance your opponent and allow you to either escape or prepare for the next rush.

Your *tai chi* teacher, Hunang, used to quote from *The Art of War* by Sun Tzu. A famed Chinese military philosopher and strategist, Sun Tzu had written more than two thousand years ago. Some of his favorite quotes were:

Great things are best accomplished when they are still easy, and wars are best won before they start.

You used to puzzle over what these things meant, and now you are beginning to understand. But how can you use both the principles of *tai chi* and the advice of a dead Chinese military philosopher?

Staying alive is your first task. Running is your strategy.

Go on to the next page.

You check your resources. You've got eighteen dollars, which isn't much in today's expensive world, an expired credit card, and a good start on the day. It's only 10:30 and the weather is warm and sunny. But your greatest asset is yourself. You are full of energy, you have a good mind and are resourceful, and the world's greatest motivators drive you: fear and the desire to survive.

"Wow! What now?" you say out loud, before realizing that your enemies might be right around the corner. Scanning the area like a fighter pilot constantly sweeping the sky for hostiles, you find the turf clear.

Okay, what will they do? you ask yourself. *Probably stake out my house, maybe watch my mom's office; they could even tap my dad's telephone. These guys play for keeps, and they have plenty of money.*

You suddenly remember the old beach house your mom's company has down on Esmeralda Bay. It's a funky old wooden place right out of the 1950s. Nobody will be there now; it's the off-season. There's canned and frozen food, and nobody will bother you—at least for a few days.

You head off in the direction of the bus stop. You will have to make at least one bus transfer to reach the coast. No sooner have you started walking than you hear an earsplitting noise.

Turn to the next page.

SLAM! SCREECH!

A cherry-red Corvette skids around the corner. It smacks into the mailbox where you were just standing, tips up on two wheels, rights itself, and speeds away.

You catch a glimpse of what looks like Sprazz in the passenger seat. But why didn't they stop? Is it a scare tactic? Are they still trying to rope you into their crummy business of trading in human misery? Your mind spins with the possibilities, and the skin on the nape of your neck prickles with the fear of sudden violence.

The Red Flowers are tracking your every move. Even the beach house may not be safe. Another option is to go to ground with an old friend whom you haven't seen in years. The friend lives in Santa Fe, New Mexico. With eighteen dollars and a useless credit card, you will have to hitchhike. That's always trouble these days with the kooks on the roads.

You hear what sounds like a car returning. You dash off to take cover behind a large bush whose scraggly, dry leaves do little to hide you.

False alarm. The car never returns.

What now? you wonder. Better make up your mind where to go.

If you decide to go to the beach house, turn to page 34.

If you decide to look up your friend Basil Ramones in Santa Fe, New Mexico, turn to page 69.

30

Faking an automobile accident is probably a good idea, you think. If you're in the hospital, the Flowers might even feel sorry for you. But despite all the skill and grace you learned in *tai chi*, you mess up big-time.

The car you pick to "nudge" you does a lot more than that.

The evening news carries a story about a young person with a tattoo of a red flower on one arm that was the victim of a hit-and-run accident at the entrance to the northbound freeway. Name unknown. Picture too ugly and horrifying to show!

The End

When you get to the hotel, you find out why the driver looks like a banker. The charge in yen for the forty-minute ride to downtown Tokyo comes out to $230 USD! The shock continues when you and your guide, who is called Sabaruki, grab a soda and a burger at the local burger hut. Price: soda, $5, burger, $12.75. At this rate you'll be on a rapid-weight-loss diet in two days.

Tons and tons of people stream by at half-run speed. The sidewalks are jammed, the shops filled, and cars choke the roads. Huge, shiny aluminum-sided buildings tower above you. Neon signs flash wherever the eye lands. But mostly you notice the noise. It sounds like a beehive in full activity. The hum of population growth out of control. Japan is a tiny group of islands with more than 120 million people. And it's still growing!

Turn to the next page.

"Hey, Sabaruki, is all of Japan this way?" you ask.

"Oh, no. Not at all. Japan is very beautiful. It has lovely countryside. It is not always so crowded, only Tokyo, and Osaka, and maybe a few other of the cities like Hiroshima and Nagasaki. And, well, even Kyoto is getting crowded." She gives you a very concerned look. You like her; you hope she is not "one of them."

"We will go to Kyoto tomorrow. That is where the big meeting is to take place. Tonight, you will rest, get over your jet lag, see a little of Japan. Tomorrow we take the Shinkansen, bullet train, to Kyoto."

"Got it," you reply, glad that there is to be a break for some badly needed sleep. The time change between LA and Tokyo is sixteen hours. Time zone changes can really throw off your whole physiological, as well as your psychological, system.

Sleep hits you like a sledgehammer, and before you know it, it's dawn! You slept right through the afternoon and evening and have awakened at 5:36 A.M. The lights of Tokyo have not quit. A reddish glow remains in the sky over the sprawling metropolis of fourteen million people, making the city look as though it were on fire.

Sabaruki meets you in the lobby of the Meridian, ready to head for Kyoto. She seems very worried and hands you a sealed envelope. "I will take care of the bill. Read this," she says.

Go on to the next page.

With trembling hands you tear open the envelope, sure that it brings bad news. You are right! The note reads:

There is no signature. In place of the signature is a chop (an ideographic symbol representing the name). You have never seen this chop before, but you have heard of it. It is the chop of a branch of the *yakuza*—a gang that is in the same business as the Flowers: human lives for sale, immigration, false passports, and if necessary, murder. They are dangerous people to deal with and maybe even more dangerous to ignore.

If you decide to ignore the letter, turn to page 59.

If you decide to take the letter seriously, turn to page 102.

34

Getting to the beach house proves easier than you thought. A friend named Tom happens by in his van, sees you, stops, and bingo! You're on your way. Tom is an old acquaintance of your family, and despite his being six years older than you, the two of you have always gotten along well. He isn't super inquisitive, as he's more concerned about himself than others. So you don't have to make up any stories.

"Thanks, Tom," you say, waving as he drives away after dropping you off. He doesn't have a good memory, so he'll soon forget having seen you.

The beach house is built between two other similar ones right on the water. The surf pounds in, and someday it will crash in and devour this house. You think it's silly that people build right where they are sure to get hit by big storms. But people all over the world do it. They build on the slopes of active volcanoes, in the paths of hurricanes and tsunamis, on earthquake fault zones, and on flood plains next to rivers. One thing about humans is they sure don't learn! At least some of them don't.

Go on to the next page.

The key is right where it always is—under the flowerpot against the wall.

The door opens. You are hit with a musty smell of disuse. Your imagination creates a decaying body. But when you step inside, the house is just as you remember it. The telephone sits on the table next to the big white couch, beckoning to you. Should you use it?

Turn to the next page.

36

You decide not to call anyone just yet. Fear sometimes generates hunger, and this is what it has done to you. You are ravenous. The freezer is stuffed with frozen pizzas, the shelves with fruit juice and boxes of spaghetti and sauces. Pizza wins. You pig out.

With night comes an offshore breeze that has the promise of a storm locked into it. Great, just what you need, a hurricane to top off the day's events. The wind howls, and the waves beat upon the beach. Sleep is difficult.

Go on to the next page.

By 2 A.M. the winds drop, the sea calms, but you are still wide awake, listening to every noise in the house. It's actually worse without the wind. Now every sound has a possible cause that can't be explained by the storm. The creak downstairs: is it Ben and Sprazz…or some other really horrible members of the gang? The scraping on the roof: is it some modern-day *ninjas* coming to get you with their small *shuriken*? The moan from the beach: is it an innocent passerby the Red Flowers are taking out so they can have a clear field while they capture you, torture you, and finally kill you by chopping you up and feeding you to the "landlord" (the surfer's name for man-eating sharks) off the beach?

None of the above! The noises are just a typical house full of moans and creaks due to age, wind, settling of the sand, and the refrigerator cycling on and off. All made frightening by your overly active imagination. But isn't it true that anything the human mind can imagine has the real possibility of existence?

Turn to the next page.

38

Your mind latches on to that last thought and follows it. Right now you wish there were a spaceship to take you away from California and away from the Red Flowers and Big Guy. Too bad thinking about it doesn't make it so.

WHAM! WHAM! WHAM! WHAM!

You hit the deck and roll, curl up in a ball, and wait for the blows that are sure to come.

Nothing. Maybe it was just a neighbor's cat knocking into some trash bins? Who knows?

Gathering your energy and bringing it down to your center—a spot called the *chi* somewhere around your navel—you prepare your mind the way Hunang taught you. It works! You feel a flow of calmness and strength, a clear mind, and preparedness for anything that is to come.

"Thank you, Hunang, thank you," you murmur. You also remember to thank yourself, for it is you, not Hunang, who is now responsible for your state of preparedness and calm.

Turn to page 41.

The police emergency number takes a long time to access. But finally you get through to an officer who talks with you in a bored voice. He takes the information and promises some action.

The action is a lonely squad car that arrives hours later. By that time, Ben, Sprazz, Big Guy, and his henchman the Anaconda are nowhere to be found. The only clue to their ever having been at the beach house is a crumpled package of chewing gum made in Hong Kong.

The police don't really believe your story and call your parents. After all, you're a kid. Why should they take you seriously?

Your dad does believe you. He is behind you. Together you convince U.S. Immigration to intercept the delivery of the cargo. It is a disaster! Big Guy anticipates everything, and the Anaconda turns the beachfront into a morgue. Bodies litter the sand, and "Big Guy" escapes. You vow to spend your life hunting this evil creature.

The End

Sleep finally comes to you like a welcome rain shower on a hot summer day. You relax into it, and the noises blend into the light rumble of the waves.

Morning arrives with two shocks: first, bright sunlight streaming into your eyes from the unshuttered bedroom window. Second, the sound of familiar voices from below.

You recognize Ben's sharp, precise voice and Sprazz and his slur and attempt to sound overly American. You shudder. How could they have tracked you down so fast?

You suddenly understand that Big Guy and his organization have ways of finding out all about anyone they want to. You've been a target from the start, you realize, with a sickness in your stomach.

Getting back into your centeredness, you creep silently to the stairwell and listen.

"Great crib, kid," Sprazz offers up. "You know, we should kidnap you, Tulip. Your parents will pay to get your back."

You feel a surge of white anger at Sprazz when he mentions the gang's nickname for you. Everyone in the Red Flowers has a flower nickname. It's supposed to confuse the cops. But you're no tulip!

Three steps more, and you bend down to listen. You can hear them clearly now. The stair creaks. You freeze. Fear starts its climb, but you use the fear to harden your resolve.

Turn to the next page.

42

"Tulip is a fool! If he were in with us, everything would be easy and the money would flow. This beach house is the best ever. Ritzy. Private. Quiet. We can bring in our cargo late at night by inflatable rafts and no one will be the wiser. Strange things happen at these fancy beach houses, and the cops are paid to keep their noses out, right, Ben?" It's Sprazz talking.

"Quiet, you spazzmatoid! Ears have walls, you know. But...yeah, you're right. The beach is *perfecto*. We'll get the first cargo tonight. There will be seventeen people in three boatloads coming in. Then there'll be another shipment of cargo next week."

Sprazz smiles wickedly. "Those shipments will be valuable. They'll be ours for years, man, years! Think of it."

"Cool it, Sprazz, or you'll end up worse off than them. Big Guy doesn't like big mouths, and don't forget where you came from."

Go on to the next page.

Slowly it becomes clear to you. The Flowers are using your mom's company's beach house as their drop-off point for the illegal immigrants from China. Their plan seems almost foolproof, but then a gang like theirs is bound to be thorough. These guys are training for the big-time crime syndicate.

They said the cargo was coming in tonight. Human lives are at stake. You've got to do something. But what? You could slip out onto the roof—it's a flat one—climb down the flower trellises, and head for help. Or you could stay and try to hear more of the plan and then alert the police.

If you decide to go for the roof now,
turn to the next page.

If you decide to wait and listen,
turn to page 47.

44

"I'm out of here!" you say silently. "Leave those creeps to the cops."

The window to the roof sticks, but you call up your energy, exert a steady pressure, focus your mind and will, and it finally gives way. You step out onto the roof, careful not to make any major noises.

Okay so far. Two steps. Hold, listen. Nothing but the occasional thump of a wave on the beach and the rush of water and sand as it retreats into the ocean.

You're at the trellis. One foot over the side. Hand on the wood, careful to avoid the rose-branch thorns. Other foot over the side. The trellis is weak and begins to wobble. You wonder which is worse, a fall to the ground and rocks below or getting caught by Ben and Sprazz and their other creepo friends.

Foot by foot, you lower yourself down the trellis. You've got about twenty feet left to go. Suddenly the humming of a car engine catches your ear. A long black limousine scrunches to a halt on the gravel and sand of the small circular drive. You cling to the trellis, trying to look like a rosebush despite the fact that you are known as Tulip.

Turn to page 46.

A gruff voice coming from the back of the limo says, "Are the boys here?"

"Yes, boss. They are. I can see them in the living room. What do you want to do?" the chauffeur asks.

"Tell them to be ready for tonight. Show Ben and Sprazz where to bring the boats in and what to do with the people. If they give you trouble, you know how to handle them. Understand?"

"Sure, boss. They've been getting too big for their sneakers anyway. I could handle them right away. We don't need them."

"Don't be hasty, Anaconda. We might need them if there's trouble. They're young and strong. There will be time for all that later."

Oh no, you think. Ben and Sprazz are going to be handled, and if your instincts are right, that means put to everlasting and permanent rest!

What to do? Should you warn them right away, or should you speed off to the cops as you originally planned? After all, Ben and Sprazz were hunting you down, and they certainly didn't mean to give you a birthday present. Live by the sword and die by the sword, isn't that the appropriate code of conduct for the likes of them? But you can't stand by and see them die.

If you decide to help Ben and Sprazz by going back inside to warn them, turn to page 18.

If you decide to leave them to their fate, turn to page 84.

You realize that the police won't believe you unless you have some hard evidence. You sneak farther down the stairs and listen to learn more.

After what seems like hours there is a knock on the door. The thug called the Anaconda enters the house.

"Okay, flower kids, this is show time!" Anaconda announces. His vicious tone sends a shiver up your spine.

Sprazz and Ben have terror in their eyes. The Anaconda is one mean guy, and they have often spoken of him with loathing. The Anaconda is known as the finisher, the pacifier, the payback man. He has a reputation for sending people on a one-way journey the Big Guy back in Japan no longer wants around.

"Hey, Conda, we're glad to see ya," Ben says with all the false courage that he can muster. You hear the fear in his voice and sense the tension through the walls and floor. This man is a messenger of evil.

Turn to the next page.

48

"Well, ain't that nice. So, you boys missed the old Anaconda. The trouble is, I didn't miss you." Anaconda isn't known for his warmth.

"Conda, we're ready and waiting," Sprazz adds in a hopeful tone. Sprazz is a coward; at least Ben isn't.

"Good, good, very good, boys. The boss will be pleased, real pleased. After the cargo is delivered, I might take you two for a little boat ride," he says, laughing. "We'll tour the beachfront. Real nice and slow. Who knows, maybe the 'landlord' is out there waiting for two nice boys like you."

You feel a chill right through to your heart. The landlord Conda refers to is the Great White shark! It is known to collect the rent from surfers. *But why would Big Guy want to get rid of Ben and Sprazz?* you ask yourself. The only answer is that Big Guy likes to limit witnesses who might one day talk and give evidence against him. An approach like this doesn't exactly inspire loyalty, but after all, these guys are criminals.

"Cargo is due at 11:20. If you perform well, then...we'll see. If you don't...well, you know what that means."

"Right, Conda. Right. We're your guys. We're cool." Ben's voice betrays his true feeling.

Go on to the next page.

Suddenly you feel a dreadful fear for them, as if it were you who faced the Anaconda, not them. What can you do? It's too late to go for help. Maybe, just maybe, you could take out Conda. You've got the advantage of concealment and surprise.

Turn to the next page.

You remember *tai chi* practice sessions with Ben and Sprazz in which the three of you devised some moves together. Your *tai chi* teacher didn't like the cooperative moves, but that didn't stop you. You even gave names to some of the moves. Grape! means to cluster around like a bunch of grapes and overwhelm your opponent; Slider! means to hit the floor and use your momentum to attack and escape. This is definitely not a *tai chi* move. It is too violent and too aggressive, but it seemed to work. The final move you practiced was called Boogie! and it involved dance-like steps and violent shouts. Again, this had nothing to do with *tai chi*. Ben and Sprazz thought up the moves. You went along just for the sake of friendship.

Conda seems to be circling Ben and Sprazz now.

So what should it be—a solo attack? Or should you yell out one of the code words to get Ben and Sprazz to attack Conda with you? Both are pretty dangerous. You could just wait and watch and witness the horror Conda has planned for them.

If you decide to attack alone,
turn to the next page.

If you decide to wait, watch, and witness,
turn to page 58.

If you decide to yell out the name of one of the
group moves, turn to page 87.

52

A solo attack! Well, heroes are born every minute.

Moving like the spider of death, you slip quietly down the stairs and enter the hallway. You extinguish all fear in your burning gut. Well, almost all fear, but a bit remains there gnawing away sending messages to your brain like: "Boy are you stupid! Kiss life goodbye!" And even "I want my momma!"

Now is the time.

You spin into the room and execute a perfect series of *tai chi* moves designed to confuse and throw off balance any adversary.

Unfortunately it doesn't work! Conda is only amused. You must have forgotten something. He stands there laughing. Then, like the snake he is named after, he strikes.

Ben and Sprazz are the witnesses to disaster, not you. You're the disaster.

The End

Sometimes taking the conservative route can be best. Reluctantly you decide to tell the police about the Red Flowers. It's a matter of a simple phone call to police headquarters.

You drop in the money, punch in the police emergency number, and wait.

"May I help you?" comes a voice.

"You sure can. I'm in trouble," you reply.

"State your name and where you are calling from. First the telephone number, then the address. Do not hang up."

You comply.

"Are you in immediate danger?" the voice asks.

Yes is your response.

"Explain, please," the voice continues.

"I can't. I need to see someone in the Rackets Department or Immigration. I need to see them now, and I need to be picked up. I'm in trouble."

"Understood. There is a squad car on the way. You are at a phone booth, correct?"

"Yes."

"Don't move, stay on the line."

"Okay, I'm here."

Turn to the next page.

Moments later a squad car pulls up. It's the most welcome sight you have ever seen. Two cops get out; they both have weapons drawn.

"Hey, kid, you all right?" the female officer asks. She smiles at you.

"I am now, Officer," you reply, moving fast to the car.

"Please, call me Stella," she says. "What's this all about, kid?"

"Blackmail, illegal immigrants, threats, and I'm really scared," you blurt out.

"Okay, we'll get you back to headquarters and they'll take it from there," Stella explains.

You sit back in the car as it moves away from the telephone booth. It takes about twenty minutes in dense traffic to get to headquarters on Eleventh Street. As you get out of the squad car, you see a black sedan roll by. Ben and Sprazz are in the car. A chill washes over you.

"Okay, here we are. Safe and sound," Stella announces.

You try to duck, hoping that Ben and Sprazz won't see you. But they have obviously followed you here. Trying to hide is useless. You enter the building, which smells of stale coffee, old newspapers, and sweat. The detectives you want to see are on the fourth floor, and the elevator creaks its way slowly upward.

It takes about twenty minutes to explain your story to three detectives, who get very excited when you mention the Red Flowers.

Turn to page 56.

"We've been after those guys for years. They're bad, real bad," the oldest of the detectives, a man named Peter Morales, says. "This could be the break we need. Kid, you might be famous. Got any guts?"

Uh-oh, you think. *Here it comes.* They want you to be some kind of hero. That's not what you had in mind.

"No, not really," you reply, trying to look weak and cowardly.

"Listen to that, will you," Peter says to his companions. "This kid's got moxie, modesty too. Just what we're looking for. Okay, here's the deal. You're the decoy. Don't worry; we'll be behind you all the way. Nothing to fear."

Your mind goes through a menu of horrifying possibilities of what the Flowers will do if they catch you. It was a mistake to come here.

"I don't think that's a good idea, Pete," one of the other detectives says. "This kid is in danger. Let's take the info and use it to bust the Red Flowers wide open."

The third detective agrees. You can tell that Pete doesn't like being overruled, but he gives in. "Okay, guess you're right. They are mean. The kid could be in trouble."

You breathe a sigh of relief. You're off the hook!

Go on to the next page.

"We'll put the kid in a safe house. Then we'll round up these thugs and the kid will testify. Okay with you?" Morales asks, looking right at you.

"Fine," you reply. "Can I call my dad?"

"Already done," one of the other detectives answers. "He's on his way down from San Francisco. He'll be here this afternoon."

Turn to page 15.

58

You decide to wait and watch. You peer into the dim room as Conda suddenly grabs each boy roughly by the arm and—

CENSORED DUE TO EXCESSIVE, GRUESOME VIOLENCE.

The End

You decide to ignore the letter. Face it, you are scared. You are involved with a Chinese gang headquartered in Japan, and a Japanese gang in Tokyo is pressuring you. Your chances for a long, peaceful life are diminishing by the day. Your decision to ignore the *yakuza* and take refuge with the Chinese gang lord Big Guy is a heavy one.

"Sabaruki, we're out of here. Let's head for Kyoto, pronto."

"Whatever you wish," she says.

Did she know what was in the letter? you ask yourself. *Maybe she is one of the* yakuza. *Boy, this is nightmare city. There isn't a place to move.* You are cornered like a cat in a dog kennel.

"Hurry, the next Shinkansen leaves in less than twenty minutes. They are always on time," she says.

Of course she is right. You make it to the rail station and board the train just as the door is about to close. The departure time is 9:22 A.M., and as the digital clock on the end of the car hits 9:22, the train moves off, accelerates, and soon is traveling at speeds in excess of 110 mph.

Turn to the next page.

60

For the next hour the train speeds through a series of cities that have almost no demarcation between them. This is the octopus-like spread of greater Tokyo. You wonder if this is a vision of the future. If it is, you want none of it.

Finally the train breaks away from the urban blight and reaches beautiful rolling countryside. Here and there you see the roofs of temples on hillsides. But that doesn't last long. Another city, more sprawl, more smokestacks, many more people. Where is the beauty of Japan?

In the midst of all this, your dilemma creeps back in. You are an unwilling accessory to crime, illegal immigration, and bribery, probably even murder. Your life is up for grabs. The Flowers have evidence implicating you and your father. Even if false it can destroy a political career. You hope the meeting will set things straight.

Go on to the next page.

Finally, the train reaches Kyoto, and Sabaruki takes you by a waiting limousine to the house of Big Guy. House is not the right term. This is a mansion on the outskirts of Kyoto, once the imperial city of ancient Japan. It is built on some of the most expensive real estate in the world. A high wall surrounds the property, along with guards, dogs, TV cameras, and monitors. But beyond the wall you find flowers, ponds, a small golf course, a stable for horses, and a garage for cars. So much beauty based on so much misery! You are at once attracted and repulsed by it.

"Come, we will meet him now," Sabaruki says. "You must show humility."

That's when it all begins to come apart!

Turn to the next page.

"Death!" a man shouts in English as he lunges from behind the bushes at the entrance of the mansion. In his hand is a knife shaped like a bird's wing. He whirls it above his head and delivers a vicious blow to Sabaruki's back. *CRAAAAK!*

You expect a shower of blood, but nothing! The man missed as she turned in a classic *tai chi* move, one of the techniques you spent hours practicing. The knife delivered a solid smack to her shoulder blades, but her actions diverted the path of the weapon, turning its face and causing a flat-sided blow. Damage: minimal.

Before you can act, Sabaruki twirls on her toes and almost dances in front of her adversary. Her movements are fluid and perfect. They seem to mesmerize the attacker, who undoubtedly knows that although he has yet to be touched, he is already a dead man.

Sure enough, two squat, broad-shouldered men in black suits and white shirts with dark blue ties appear as if out of the woodwork of the mansion. One of the black suits delivers a vicious *karate* chop to the attacker. The other black suit lets fly with an equally vicious kick to his lower jaw. There is a sudden cracking sound, and then a thud as he falls. The attacker lies on the ground like a sack of potatoes. Sabaruki walks over him as if he weren't there. You decide to be wary of her.

Turn to page 65.

The day proceeds as though nothing had happened! Life and death appear to mean nothing to these people. The attacker—who knows who he was, a *yakuza*—is trundled away like fresh-cut grass and dumped where no one will find him. You are led into a library to wait until Big Guy will see you.

Almost an hour later, when you have begun to really sweat it out, Sabaruki returns, calm as ever, and motions you to follow her.

Big Guy is in his special chamber, an office built entirely of jade. The green glow of the jade suffuses the room with a tremulous light. You take one look at the leader of the Red Flowers and feel like vomiting. Big Guy has no head! Instead he sports a small crystal globe with what looks like computer innards. One mechanical eye scans the room, and a pair of artificial lips seems to moisten themselves. He, or it, speaks.

"Horrible, aren't I? Repulsive, frightening, disgusting. But nonetheless marvelous! I think, I act, and I LIVE." His hands reach down—they are real hands on real arms—and lift a head made of soft, pliable plastic. The hands set the head over the globe and secure it to the shoulders with two Velcro straps. "Now I'm ready. I just wanted to show you, my young friend, that I have a will larger than anyone or anything this world could imagine!"

Turn to the next page.

You can't help but stare. Your parents have always told you not to stare at people with deformations or injuries, but you can't stop looking.

"Go ahead, enjoy yourself. I fascinate myself. Yes, I have lost my head, crushed in an accident arranged by my enemies, or you might say my competitors. They probably sent the man at the door that attacked my daughter. They never give up; but that keeps life interesting, don't you think?"

You are at a loss for words.

"Never mind. I didn't expect an answer. Now, let's get down to business. You have come here to speak for your father. He is in a position to open doors for me and protect me from the immigration authorities. You could say that his help would be humanitarian. There are just too many people in China; over 1.4 billion of them, and growing like a pond full of tadpoles in the early summer. We just help some of the more deserving ones go to America. America needs these people. And your father will be well paid."

You mumble an inaudible comment. Big Guy takes it for an affirmative.

"So, you convince your father to help, and we in turn will help both him and you. We can even arrange to help your mother. We are reasonable people. Think of us as friends, and look upon us as relatives. You will inherit much from us. The Flowers offer membership in a powerful group much like a family. You will never be alone, and you will never have to worry about money."

Go on to the next page.

"But what if he won't agree to help?" you ask. Your heart seems to be bumping up against your throat. Scanning the room, you see that the only occupants are you, Big Guy, and Sabaruki. No guards. Obviously you are not seen as any threat.

"Well, that would be a problem. We might have to send him a reminder. Maybe a little piece of you would suffice. Oh, no, dear child, do not fear. It would only be a little piece, a very little piece. A fingertip. An earlobe. I'm sure your father is reasonable and will agree right away. Don't let it worry your head one bit."

The reality of the situation comes down with the ferocity of an avalanche. You are a hostage. You have been kidnapped. Kidnapped by yourself. You got on the plane, you came to Japan. You made yourself a hostage. The ransom is awesome: your dad's career and probably his life. These people will never let go. They are bloodsuckers.

If you attack Big Guy right this minute, turn to the next page.

If you agree to try and get your dad to help, turn to page 76.

Tai chi is not an attack skill; it is a defensive skill that uses the opponent's energy to your benefit. So you revert to sheer aggression. This is the tool that most species use.

With a yell loud enough to awaken the dead, you lunge at Big Guy and, with a ferocious swipe of your hand, you dislodge the globe over the computer head. It drops to the floor and smashes.

But Big Guy has more up his sleeve than that. He swivels the still-operating electronic eye, and a ray of laser light stabs the air, then blasts through you. You feel your energy slip away like water in a sink with the drain open.

"You cannot defeat me," Big Guy says with an evil laugh. "I am all-powerful and the world will soon be mine."

Those are the last words you ever hear.

The End

You decide to get as far away from here as possible. *Santa Fe is supposed to be quite a place,* you say to yourself. *There are rich people, famous people, not-so-famous people, and a lot of ex-hippies. Lots of people in the film community also hang out there. It is quite the melting pot,* you think to yourself. *What better place to try and melt right in?*

Basil Ramones is none of the above. He is a kid from Florida whose dad and mom moved to New Mexico to work in the computer industry. Computer stuff is really big out there. You know him from summer camp two years ago.

"Basil, here I come!" you shout out loud.

A Number 12 bus would take you out to good old Route 66. It would head off through the desert and eventually go through Santa Fe, along through other towns like Las Vegas, Nevada, and Phoenix, Arizona.

"Thumb, get ready for work," you say, and you plant yourself on the highway and hope that you get a nice, safe, nonstop ride to the bus station.

One hour zips by.

Then another thirty minutes.

Nothing happens. No cars stop. *Who wants to pick up some kid?* you think. You wish you had a pocketful of money. Here you are in a jam with no cashola. Things look grim.

Turn to page 71.

Finally an eighteen wheeler pulls to a wheezing, dusty stop, and the driver jumps out. She's about forty-five, red-haired, with lots of jewelry on her wrists.

"Hey, kid, what ya doin' out here? Highways are dangerous. Don't you know that? Didn't your mom teach you nothin'?" she shouts over the roar of traffic.

"I'm sorry, ma'am, I didn't mean any harm," you say, getting into the semi-grovel. It's a technique to make parents and other adults feel really bad that they made you feel bad. It's a surefire worker, and this time is no exception.

"Hey, my name's Fran, and I'm a friend out here. No ma'amin' me. Hop aboard and we'll boogie. Whasss your final destination?"

"Santa Fe, Fran."

"Runnin' away from home, are ya?" she asks.

"Well, not really," is your evasive reply. A thousand great lies pop into your brain as you climb into the cab of the truck: my brother's in jail and I need to bail him out; my dad's a millionaire and doesn't give me a cent, but I want to see him; I'm on a treasure hunt that ends up in Santa Fe; if I get there first I win a million dollars; I just love the road, travelin's my bag; and the final, my mom's dying, I've just got to get there before she goes.

But you don't try any of these. Fran's no dope. She'd see right through you. Just at that moment you glance in the side-view mirror and see the red Corvette speeding down the road. It's catching up fast!

Turn to the next page.

You sink down in your seat so those in the car can't see you, whoever they are. None of them look like killers, but after all, what do killers really look like?

In your heart you know it's probably Sprazzle and Ben or at least their cohorts.

"What's up, dude?" Fran says, trying to use slang. It doesn't fit too well with her, but you appreciate the attempt.

"Nothing. Absolutely nothing," you reply.

"Sure, sure, nothin'. Is that why you look as white as pizza dough and all scrunched up in that seat? Jeez, even a state cop couldn't find you without a flashlight. Be straight with me."

"Okay, Fran, this is the story: those guys in the car are after me. I can't tell you why. I'm in deep trouble, and I'm not the cause."

"Fair enough," she says, and scans the rear-view mirror. The car is still playing tag. "I've got my own troubles, kid, but…what the heck."

Your mind catalogs the possibilities, and they are not nice. Sprazzle could call ahead and arrange a hostile greeting party. Ben could unleash untold damage on the truck, Fran, and you. Or they could bide their time, wait for the truck to stop, and then "hit" you. You turn to Fran. "I'm sorry I got you into this, Fran. I'm real sorry." You don't know what else to say.

"Let's not be sorry, let's just figure a way out," Fran replies.

Go on to the next page.

"There's nothing to figure," you say glumly. "They're there, and I'm here. I'm a sitting duck."

"Not yet. I've got a trick or two up my sleeve," Fran says, reaching over and picking up the CB mike. "Hey, out there in La La Land, listen up. This is Big Fran in a silver roadrunner headed east on Route 66, about fifteen miles due west of Eldorado. I've got rats on my tail and I'm not talking blue hats."

Fran must be referring to state troopers, you think to yourself.

"These guys are for real and they're bad news. Come on back to me and give me backup," Fran says, releasing the CB button.

Turn to the next page.

Fran settles herself in the big leather seat that looks like a chair in an air-force rocket-launch command center. She grins at you, stomps down on the big accelerator, and says, "Watch this!" She leans on the air horns, which give a blast like a giant transatlantic ocean liner entering New York Harbor, and begins rapidly switching lanes.

The CB opens up. "Okay, Big Fran, this here is Mighty Mouse comin' up fast on yer tail. Who's the pest?"

"Big Fran comin' back at ya, Mighty—red Corvette, two guys, they are to be considered armed and dangerous."

"No *problema*, Fran. Mighty Mouse will stick to them like a burr to a bear."

You see a dusty, rattling old eighteen wheeler loaded to the McGillicuddies with squashed car bodies sidle up to Fran's rig. Mighty Mouse waves and nods, then switches lanes and rides abreast of Fran. Sprazz and Ben are caught behind the two monster trucks and can't do much.

Turn to page 82.

76

With a very heavy heart you say, "Okay, I'll get in touch with my dad, but I don't think he'll help you. He's tough."

"Very good, my young friend. But when it comes to children, parents will do most anything for them. Someday you will realize that yourself, when you have your own children. Look at this as a business deal between businessmen. You are just the link, the conduit, the middleman. You will be rewarded, have no fear. We are generous to those who help and remain loyal. Relax now and have my daughter show you around.

"Tonight, we will contact your father through our own independent satellite link. We bought the satellite from the French. No one can interrupt our signal. It's better than any system the Americans have. It is totally secure. Some of the drug lords in South America want a similar system, but they will never get it. They are too greedy, too violent. Well, off with you. Till tonight."

Go on to the next page.

Almost in a trance from the rush of events, you allow Sabaruki to lead you away. You soon find yourself in another chauffeured car that winds its way through tiny, crowded streets and ends up at a large set of gates on the outskirts of the city. Mountains surround the area.

"This is Shugakuin," says Sabaruki. "It was the summer palace of an emperor who preferred to reside here in quiet. He allowed the *shogunate*—fierce warlords—to rule the country. It was of course sad for the country. But then that was the decision of the emperor. In reality he was a prisoner of the *shogunate*."

Turn to the next page.

The summer palace is one of the most beautiful places you have ever seen. It is composed of three small buildings, each more delicate and perfect than the last. They stretch up a wooded and flowered hillside that overlooks a beautiful man-made lake. It is elegant, simple, and exquisite.

When you reach the highest point Sabaruki pulls you aside.

"I am not his daughter. I am a slave! Big Guy has no children. He kidnapped me in Hong Kong when I was four years old and raised me as his daughter. Despite his kindness, I fear and loathe him. I hate what he does. To him money is a god and people are mere objects. He would kill you in an instant if he thought you were of no use to him.

He is powerful. Many people are beholden to him in governments and businesses around the world. His plan is to become emperor of China and ruler of the entire world. He is mad!"

You are stunned. The rest of the Red Flowers seem like a play group compared to this egomaniac with a computerized brain. *What can you do?* you ask yourself. Before you can think of anything, Sabaruki speaks.

"I have a plan. It is a dangerous plan, but we might succeed in stopping this madness. Will you join me?"

"I don't know. I don't really have too many choices. What is your plan?"

Turn to the next page.

80

"Very simple," she replies. "We kidnap Big Guy and hold him hostage."

"Are you crazy? We'll never get away with it. There are guards all over the place. We'll be mincemeat in minutes. Think again, Sabaruki, think again."

"You Americans are always so hasty in making judgments. You have not listened to my plan."

"So, I'm all ears," you answer. "What is it?"

"I am very competent in computers. A computer program rules his life. Without it, he will die."

"So what? We don't have the program. He does."

"Be silent. You think like a child. He wants upgrades to his program for life support. I am the only technician trusted with this vital work. I will replace the current program with an altered program. It will put him in our power."

"Awesome! How do I come in?" you ask.

"You will arrange a deal in the United States for the return of my two brothers. They are slaves of the Red Flowers. They have been programmed by this monster to be criminals. I want them to come back to Hong Kong. I want them to be normal. I love them."

"Who are they?" you ask, half dreading the reply.

"They are called Ben and Sprazz, but to me they are Jing and Little Pebble. You must have your father help them."

Go on to the next page.

Blood turns to ice in your veins; muscle turns to putty; fear becomes reality. Ben and Sprazz! Brothers of Sabaruki. Could the moon become the sun and the sun become the bottom of the sea? NO, NO, NO! You hope that this is all some malignant nightmare and that you will wake up in your own bed back in the good old U S of A.

No such luck. Sabaruki awaits your reply.

"Okay, I'm in. But—and this is a big but— where do we go once we kill Big Guy? Who will take us in?"

"I have friends in the *yakuza*. They will take us in. They hate him. They hate him big-time."

"Okay, what do I do now?" you ask.

"Ask for a meeting with him," she replies. "Ask for an immediate meeting, alone. You will distract him while I begin the reprogramming."

You think for a moment. Ben and Sprazz have double-crossed you before. Maybe Sabaruki will do the same. But she is right about one thing: Big Guy will almost certainly kill you after he is done using you.

*If you go along with this scheme,
turn to page 25.*

*If you decide to inform Big Guy and hope for a
favor in return, turn to page 110.*

The CB crackles again.

"Hey, Fran, it's Doodle Bug and the Big Bad Ten. I hear ya, and I'm going to see that the car stays right where we want it."

"Thanks, Doodle. We'll need some help at the next rest stop. Are you with me?" Fran asks.

"Like flies on apple pie, Fran," Doodle replies.

"Count me in," Mighty adds, and soon there are offers of help coming in from almost every truck on the road. You begin to relax. Maybe you'll make it after all.

"Hey, kid! We got you covered real good. What next? I mean this rig needs fuel, we need food, and what are we goin' to do with you? You want the blue hats in on this?" Fran of course means the state troopers.

"No, no! No cops!" you say, really upset and excited. "Not now."

"Kid, what kind of trouble are you in anyway? I'm sticking my neck out, and you're not playin' real fair with me," Fran replies, giving you a serious look with one eye as she scans the road with the other. Her rig is pushing seventy, and there is a strong wind blowing.

Go on to the next page.

You wonder whether you should let her in on the whole mess. It might end up hurting her. The Red Flowers and the Big Guy in Japan are not known for being kind to anyone who is out to do them dirt. On the other hand, Fran already is involved.

What to do? The same question always comes hurtling back at you.

*If you decide to tell Fran all about it,
turn to page 92.*

*If you decide to keep quiet, get off at the truck
stop, and try to slip away on your own,
turn to page 96.*

"I'll leave them to their own fate," you say to yourself, despite feeling a tinge of guilt. After all, these two creeps have messed up your life big-time with no regrets. To them you are just a commodity to be used and discarded like a fast food container. *Let them get what they deserve,* you think.

The Anaconda is big and agile. You watch him carefully, trying to assess how smart he is, how quick with mind and body. What are your chances of escape? What is the advantage of speed over stealth?

Your heart pounds so loudly you think the thug must hear it; your breathing seems to echo.

"Now!" you say to yourself, as you slide across the space between the beach house and the hedge that separates it from the neighbors'.

So far, so good. You hunker down and try to become a shadow. You turn your mind to a wavelength where body and energy blend. You think shadow and become shadow. The thug scans the area with his eyes, but they are not seeing eyes. They bump over the place where you lie, never noticing your form in the lee of the shrubs.

You time your breath with your heartbeat. You are breathing once for every two and a half beats. On a count of five breaths, you rise from the shadows of the shrubs. You dart out from behind them, and then simply walk away.

Courage flows through you, and you keep on going. With each step you are farther away from the terror and the knowledge of the shortness of life. The future is beginning to look good.

"Police, here I come," you say to yourself.

You're across the road, down the street, and still no pursuit. You reach a house several blocks away and scramble up the steps. You knock on the door. Once, twice, tentatively. Then twice more with force.

"Scram!" comes a mean voice. "Scram, or I'll blow you away," the voice says.

You imagine a man holding a very large handgun filled with very large and nasty bullets.

"I need help," you muster in a squeaky voice.

"You'll need more than help unless you make tracks."

Turn to the next page.

"Please!" You're almost shouting now. "I need help!"

There is no noise for a moment. Then the door opens a crack, held in check by a very heavy chain.

"What kind of help?" says a frail voice. The tough guy act is gone.

"Police. I want to report a crime about to happen. I need your phone," you say. Something in your voice must communicate your anxiety and also your trustworthiness, because the chain slips from its holder and the door opens to reveal a kid about your age. He holds a water zapper in his hands.

"Okay, but don't try any funny stuff, got it?" he says.

"Sure, sure. No problem."

Turn to page 39.

Three of you should be able to take out the Anaconda.

"Grapes!" you yell, leaping into the room like one of the famous Bardolini Brothers flying-trapeze artists.

"Grapes!" you yell again.

But Ben and Sprazz just stand there with their mouths open.

"GRAPES! GRAPES! GRAPES! You idiots!"

Conda laughs his deep, dirty chuckle. Time freezes. Your heart pounds like a drum roll.

As if in slow motion, Conda advances toward you, grinning.

Instinctively you raise your hands, crooking the wrists. Then you drop them as though they were parachutes falling to earth. On the balls of your feet you turn toward Conda and execute a circling movement with your hands as though you were embracing a miniature Earth globe.

Conda rushes you, yelling and screaming in a high-pitched atavistic voice, anger and hatred and violence pouring out of him.

You continue your slow, rhythmic movements, as though taking the globe of Earth and moving it gracefully.

Awareness. Calmness. Centeredness.

Conda continues his rush.

You take his energy and turn it to the side, allowing the man to pass you in a flurry of arms and kicking legs.

Turn to the next page.

WHAP! Conda hits the wall and is stunned. Ben and Sprazz recover from their shock and fly onto him like bees to a ripe flower.

Moments later Conda is a prisoner. Ben and Sprazz tie him up with nylon boat line they brought for the landing tonight.

"What about Big Guy?" you ask.

"Yes, what about me?" Big Guy says, appearing in the doorway. He is dressed in an ancient robe and has a large head that looks unnatural. "Be so kind as to untie this unfortunate buffoon who used to be called Anaconda. I think we will now call him Shark Food."

"No, boss! No, please. It was their fault, not mine!" Conda says in a pleading tone. "Remember, boss, I saved your life back in Shanghai. Don't forget me," Conda pleads.

"I do not forget. I am just making arrangements for you to join your venerable ancestors a little ahead of schedule, Conda. You should have better manners and thank me." Big Guy is laughing now.

That's when you hit him! Leaping from the ground like a skateboard rat, you take Big Guy in the chest and send him flying! Once again Ben and Sprazz do their thing. Soon Big Guy is trussed up like a pig and sitting next to Conda.

"We're outta here," Sprazz says with great force as he and Ben race for the door.

Turn to page 109.

90

You hide the package and mess up your clothes as if you had been in a fight. Now it's time to report to Ben and Sprazz that the package has been stolen. You are a terrible liar. No matter how hard you try, people can see it written all over your face when you try even a mild form of bending the truth. Still, you do your best some forty minutes later when you face your two erstwhile friends.

Go on to the next page.

"Honest, guys, you wouldn't believe what happened," you say.

"Try us, you might be surprised," Ben says. His arms are folded across his chest in a hostile manner.

"Well, I was walking along just minding my own business when this kid comes up to me. A real mean-looking guy, you know. He had a sinister look about him, especially around the eyes."

"Sounds like some guys we know, right, Ben?" Sprazz says. "So, you just hand the kid the package, without him even asking for it? Is that it?"

"No way! I'm no pushover! I tried to talk him out of it, I tried to evade him, I tried to tell him who he was messin' with…honest! I did everything I could." Your face and nose begin to twitch with the sure signs of your lying. Sweat gathers on your neck.

Ben and Sprazz push you to the ground. Sprazz kicks you.

"Too bad for you, Tulip. If the package doesn't get to where it belongs, then you are going to get where you deserve to belong! Bing, bang, bong!" Ben does not smile. "Come with us. You've got an appointment to keep."

Big Guy is crueler than you imagined. You're finished!

The End

One thing that your *tai chi* master always stressed was to take advantage of the situation at hand, be prepared, and use the energy coming your way. Well, when you add it all up, Fran is energy coming your way to help. She needs to be prepared for what is really going on to be truly effective, and you must use the opportunities as they present themselves to you. You decide to tell Fran the whole story, start to finish.

Fran doesn't say much for the next fifteen minutes as you tell her your story. She occasionally talks with one of the seven rigs providing a protective cordon around you, but she pays attention and gives her take when you are finished.

"Well, kid, we got two problems: first your safety. Nobody is gonna harm you. Over my dead body. Okay. So, we're on to *número* two in the problem area. The way I see it is these dirtbags are dealin' in human flesh. I feel for those poor people tryin' their best to get a new life here in the good old U S of A. I know a lot of them end up as slaves to these gangs. We got to stop it."

"But Fran, how? I'm just a kid and you're—"

"Just a truck driver and a woman to boot, is that what you mean? No way, we're people, and age means nothin'. I've got friends and you've got your dad and mom. My ex is a cop. We'll handle these creeps, you can bet on it."

Go on to the next page.

Before you can prevent her, Fran is on the CB again, and this time she asks for a patch to the state police. It happens fast.

"Get me Detective Sam Carbone. Yeah, this is his ex, but what I'm talking about is really important. No…it's not personal."

A minute or two passes. Then, "Fran, what is it? What's up?"

"Need you bad, Sam. Got a young adult here with me who is onto the Red Flowers gang and the scam for bringin' in poor Chinese people for a price and a life of near slavery. We've got two goons on our tail. Do you read me?"

"Like a book, Fran. We know the Red Flowers; they're bad, very bad. You need help and fast."

"Talk to me, baby. Oops, sorry about that, Sam, know you don't like to be called baby."

"Forgiven and forgotten. Listen close, Fran. I'm sending helicopters to cover you and patrol cars to set up a roadblock. Meanwhile, put that kid on the radio. We need the info. We've been waiting for a break on this gang for months. This could be it."

You get on the CB and give all the information you possibly can to Detective Sam Carbone. Suddenly you feel that the support net that society offers to all its citizens has opened up and taken you in. You are not alone, not just a kid in trouble, but a person receiving help from other people and from society. You are filled with hope.

Turn to the next page.

94

A nagging fear intrudes on your newfound peace: can your patch to the police be heard by anyone with a CB? If so, you have just broadcast your story to the world. The Red Flowers are powerful, and you've just ratted on them. They'll hunt you until the day you die.

Fran reads your mind. "Relax, kid. My CB has a police scramble. Sam installed it for me. Your transmission is safe. Let's get on with it."

Get on with it you do. About twenty miles up the road, the state police set up a block. When the rigs pull onto the shoulder, the car is quickly surrounded. Ben and Sprazzle are captured and led away in handcuffs. A police chopper transports you to Los Angeles for a meeting with the district attorney and a collection of officials and detectives.

The net that protected you is now going to scoop up the gang members and protect society from them. Everything looks like it's going to go well…except that Big Guy is still holed up in his fabulous palace on the outskirts of Kyoto in Japan. The Red Flowers are only one of this super crook's many operations. You'd better be prepared, better use opportunity as it comes, and better keep your eyes and ears open.

Turn to page 108.

You stay quiet and stare down at your arm. The initiation tattoo revolts you now, but it reminds you that the Flowers are bad guys! They deal in human flesh cloaked in the guise of hope.

So, with a backpack full of guilt that weighs you down, you decide not to involve this warm and friendly trucker. You'll get off at the truck stop and slip away. You take courage in the teachings of your *tai chi* master and remember him saying, "You can do things way beyond what you believe you can do. Use your energy, use others' energy, and stay poised, ready, and confident. Let the event unravel the way you want it to without forcing it."

"Fran, I can't tell you anything. It's too dangerous...for me as well as for you."

"Hey, kid, I've been around a long time and plan on stayin' around even more. Don't tell me if you don't want to, but I can help. I'm sure of that. Old Fran knows a thing or two."

You sigh. Here you are hurtling along an interstate escorted by a band of truckers, with thugs in a cherry-red Corvette trying to get at you and finish your days on good old planet Earth. How are you going to put her off?

Turn to the next page.

"Fran, let's talk the whole thing over at the truck stop. I'll tell you then," you say, knowing that you aren't going to tell her a thing. You hate being a liar, but this is for a good cause.

"Okay, truck stop coming up in about eight miles. Hang tight."

Sure enough, the truck stop emerges out of nowhere in the middle of the desert in eight minutes. With a lot of downshifting, the great truck slows, turns off the highway, and finally nudges into a free space. Your escort convoy picks spots nearby. The red Corvette is nowhere to be seen! Your heart skips a couple of beats. *Where could they be?* you wonder.

"Okay, follow me," Fran says as she opens the door and climbs down to the gravel of the parking area, "I'll watch for them. So will the others."

The best thing to do is to slip away right now. You spot a bus loading up passengers for Santa Fe. You dash off between three big eighteen wheelers before Fran can do anything. You just don't want others getting hurt. This is your gambit. You'll play it out by yourself.

So far, so good. You hide behind a truck and look around carefully. The way is clear, so you sprint for the next one. The bus is in sight, and you still have most of your eighteen dollars. It won't get you to Santa Fe, but it will buy you time and distance.

Go on to the next page.

You climb aboard the bus. It's about half full. The driver sits in his seat picking his teeth.

"Where to, kid?" he asks.

"Ah, c-can I see the schedule?" you stammer.

"Sure, here," he says and hands you a schedule, then returns to his tooth picking.

Fourteen ninety-five will get you to a town called Nevers, Nevada. It will have to do, you decide.

"Nevers," you say, handing over fifteen dollars. He takes it, gives you a nickel change, and pays no more attention to you. *That's good,* you think. *The less people notice you, the better.*

Moments later the bus leaves, and you settle back, regretting that you never told Fran the truth. Someday, somewhere, you will, you decide, looking back at her rig. She is standing by it with a bewildered look on her face. Sadness fills you.

A hand reaches over the seat from behind you. It taps your shoulder. When you slowly turn around, you see Sprazz smiling an evil smile.

Turn to page 101.

"Change of plans, pal. We get off in Phoenix. We have a really nice reception waiting for you. You'll never forget it." Sprazz chuckles and pops gum into his mouth. The bus is on its way. Sprazz moves forward and sits next to you. Across the aisle, reading a newspaper, is Ben. He lowers the paper and grins. You never get to see Basil in Santa Fe. You never get to see your family again. A mound of sand in the desert is your last resting place.

The End

102

The *yakuza* are very powerful. You decide to obey their wishes. The Road of the Yellow Fish is near the fish market in Tokyo. A taxi charging exorbitant rates delivers you to the heart of the market. It is a piece of old Japan, unchanged for centuries. Noodle shops line the sidewalks filled with hungry people slurping the rich broth and fresh noodles.

You wish you could stop and investigate this wonderful area, but life and death—yours—might well hang in the balance. You approach number 231, and to your surprise find a modern house in excellent condition. It looks incongruous next to the old shops and stores and stalls.

You knock. No answer. You wait, and then knock again.

When the door opens, a short, very fat woman greets you.

"Please to come in," she says in broken English. "Follow me." The woman leads you to the back of the house. Without warning, a large fishnet drops over your head, entangling you in web. *Why me? Why me? I didn't do anything...*

Go on to the next page.

Three weeks later, your father and mother sit in the office of the deputy commissioner of police for Los Angeles. "I am sorry to report that we have absolutely no leads regarding the whereabouts of your child. I can offer you little hope, but we will keep on trying."

Unfortunately, *yakuza* victims are never found.

The End

104

You decide to chuck the package. It symbolizes all the trouble these thugs have caused you. What you hate most is the trafficking of human lives that these people depend on for their money...maybe even their kicks in life. You remind yourself to be careful from now on in picking your friends. But you also pledge that you won't distrust everyone you meet. You'll just take a little more time, ask more questions, and take care judging people.

"Okay, let's do it!" you say in a half whisper as you approach a convenience store. You see a dumpster parked next to it in a lot filled with a collection of junk. "So long!" you say more loudly as you pitch the hated package into the air and watch its slow trajectory into the dumpster.

Free of this evil thing, your footsteps lighten, your head picks up, and your mood changes. "Just let them try anything," you say. "This is America. It's safe here."

Three blocks later, you turn the corner—and scream!

Ben and Sprazz stand there, legs akimbo, nasty smiles on their faces.

"So, if it isn't our own delivery service. Well, isn't that sweet. How about the guarantee, Ben? No package delivered, no life to lead, right?"

"You got it, Sprazz. I don't see the package, do you?"

Go on to the next page.

"Not unless he shrink-wrapped it, Ben. How about it, Tulip, did you deliver the package like a good messenger? Or did you throw it in the dumpster back there like a nasty person who betrays his friends? Is this it?" Sprazz holds up the package.

"Tulip better come with us. Perhaps a meeting with the Anaconda will make him remember that the pledge of all the Red Flowers is question not. Act, don't think. The leader is all-powerful."

You try to melt into the sidewalk. No luck. You're a goner, and you know it. What would your *tai chi* master say now? What would he suggest?

Concentrate. Center.

In a flash you grab the package out of the hands of the startled Sprazz. Your attention and awareness are complete. Your feet respond to all the neural transmitters that are urgently telling them to flee.

You run down the street, around the corner. Ben and Sprazz are probably behind you, but you don't care. Your body and mind are one; you are running toward freedom, toward honor—

Red light! Traffic stopped!

You dash across the intersection of Bosworth and Strobe, a main drag.

Turn to page 107.

A cop car is parked there! Never have the black and white of a police cruiser looked so warm and inviting!

Flinging open the rear door, you collapse into the car, startling the two police officers.

"Take me to headquarters!" you exclaim. "Quick, they're after me!"

The cops turn and look at you as though you had lost your marbles. "And who may we say is calling?" the older one asks.

"If you want to get a promotion by nailing the Red Flowers gang, let's get going," you reply.

"Red Flowers?" one cop asks incredulously. He eyes his partner. "Floor it!"

You clutch the package in your hands. Outside the car a very angry twosome of Ben and Sprazz try to act like casual passersby. Ben shoots you a look of hatred, but the cruiser is on the move, headed for the police station.

The package contains $100,000, an attempt by the Red Flowers to bribe the governor. It, and your testimony, is enough evidence to have the gang captured and put on trial. May the wheels of justice deliver this time!

The End

108

It's a witness protection program for you for the next couple of years, but it won't be so bad. You're still a kid and things will change. You pack your bag and move to Hawaii. Surf's up!

As for Ben and Sprazz, they are doing time and will be for quite a while.

The End

"I'll get you!" Big Guy shouts after them.

"Maybe, maybe not," you say to him as you stand at the telephone dialing the police emergency number.

Somewhere off the coast is a small tramp steamer riding high in the water because its only cargo is six important Chinese men. When it drops anchor, two 12-foot Zodiacs are lowered and set out for shore. The police will soon greet the passengers.

The End

110

Feeling like a creep and a traitor because you are betraying Sabaruki, you approach the jade room where Big Guy stays. Your heart pulses as fast as a drum roll for a heavy-metal band. Your hands are clammy. You feel like vomiting.

You step into the chamber. "What is it?" asks Big Guy.

"I have information for you that I believe is valuable," you reply.

"Ah, my young one, you are already learning the game, aren't you? Seductive, isn't it, power over people? What is it you have learned?"

You hesitate; there is still a chance to back away from this betrayal. But survival instincts propel you forward. "I know of a traitor within your group." You wait.

Big Guy does not move. He doesn't have his artificial head on at this time, and you can see the obscene single electronic eye and the guts of the computer clearly. "Tell me."

"No! First a deal and then the information," you shoot back, surprised at your boldness.

"Ha, ha, ha! You have the makings of a good one—or perhaps a bad one. What do you want?"

Go on to the next page.

"My freedom and the same for my dad. Simple. If what I have to tell you isn't worth it, then do what you wish."

Big Guy ponders this for several moments. His electronic eye swivels in a scanning pattern about the room.

"Okay. Cards up. Enlighten me," he says.

Turn to page 113.

You take a deep breath and then speak. "Sabaruki is the traitor. She is preparing to alter your computer program so that she may hold you in her power. She will then turn you over to your enemies in the *yakuza*."

The single eye flutters and then shuts down. A moaning fills the room. The light from the computer in the globe on top of Big Guy's shoulders quits.

Silence.

You wonder if Big Guy is dead. The glow of the jade room seems to intensify. A door slides open behind him. Sabaruki steps in. Her face is animated. She smiles strangely and speaks.

"You played your role well. I knew the shock of your message would short-circuit his delicate sensibilities. Now I will change the program card, and he is in my absolute power. As for you, we'll deal with you later."

She removes the globe, takes out a computer card, and prepares to insert the altered program. It's your one and only chance. You leap at her, knocking her to one side and grab both cards. Sabaruki falls hard onto the floor and begins moaning wildly. She is grabbing her ankle and flopping back and forth. Without a second lost, you continue your motion and sprint to the door.

You make it to the street and keep running. You're going to make it back home, you're sure of it now. The future might be uncertain if Sabaruki seeks revenge, but at least for now you have a future.

The End

ABOUT THE ARTIST

Ilustrator: Marco Cannella was born in Ascoli Piceno, Italy on September 29, 1972. Marco started his career in art as decorator and illustrator when he was a college student. He became a full-time professional in 2001 when he received the flag-prize for the "Palio della Quintana" (one of the most important Italian historical games). Since then, he has worked as illustrator for the Studio Inventario in Bologna. He has also worked as scenery designer for professional theater companies. He works for the production company ASP SRL in Rome as character designer and set designer on the preproduction of a CG feature film. In 2004 he moved to Banglore, India to work full-time on this project as art director.

ABOUT THE AUTHOR

R. A. Montgomery attended Hopkins Grammar School, Williston-Northampton School and Williams College where he graduated in 1958. Montgomery was an adventurer all his life, climbing mountains in the Himalaya, skiing throughout Europe, and scuba-diving wherever he could. His interests included education, macro-economics, geo-politics, mythology, history, mystery novels, and music. He wrote his first interactive book, *Journey Under the Sea*, in 1976 and published it under the series name *The Adventures of You*. A few years later Bantam Books bought this book and gave Montgomery a contract for five more, to inaugurate their new children's publishing division. Bantam renamed the series *Choose Your Own Adventure* and a publishing phenomenon was born. The series has sold more than 260 million copies in over 40 languages.

For games, activities, and other fun stuff, or to write to Chooseco, visit us online at CYOA.com

Tattoo of Death Trivia Quiz

Hopefully you were successful in one of the most dangerous adventures. The Red Flowers are tough —are you tougher?

1) *Tai Chi* is an ancient Chinese martial art that stresses what rather than attack?
   A. Weapon Choice
   B. Defense
   C. Shouting and moving your arms around
   D. Offense

2) Hunang Fanng tells you to imagine your arms are
   A. Swords
   B. Guns
   C. Lotus Leaves
   D. Parachutes

3) Big Guy lives in the city of
   A. Los Angeles, California
   B. Tokyo, Japan
   C. Kyoto, Japan
   D. Beijing, China

4) The Red Flowers force you to deliver a package with a photograph that proves _____ is a criminal
   A. Your dog
   B. The governor
   C. Your science teacher
   D. King Kong

5) Who are Doodle Bug, Mighty Mouse, and Big Fran?
   A. Trained squirrels who deliver messages in Japan
   B. *Tai Chi* masters who are rude to you in Los Angeles
   C. Truck drivers who help you on the way to New Mexico
   D. Gang members who were kicked out for having dumb names

6) When you tell the police about the Red Flowers, they ask you to
   A. Become a decoy
   B. Go on television
   C. Go home because you must be lying
   D. Go to jail

7) Who is "the landlord"?
   A. A gangster who lives by the beach
   B. A singer in a night club
   C. A dog that attacks people in the beach house
   D. A shark that eats surfers

8) What are Grape! Slider! and Boogie!?
   A. *Tai Chi* moves you made up
   B. Your favorite restaurants in California
   C. Secret weapons used on Big Guy
   D. Your parents' nicknames for you and your brothers

9) Who is Tulip?
   A. Your favorite gangster
   B. A fashion designer you meet in Los Angeles
   C. A helpful koala bear
   D. You!

10) What move overtakes both Big Guy and Anaconda?
   A. Jelly
   B. Peanut Butter
   C. Grape
   D. Slider

CHOOSE YOUR OWN ADVENTURE® 1

THE ABOMINABLE SNOWMAN

CHOOSE FROM 28 ENDINGS!

BY R. A. MONTGOMERY

CHOOSE YOUR OWN ADVENTURE® 2

JOURNEY
UNDER THE SEA

CHOOSE FROM 42 ENDINGS

BY R. A. MONTGOMERY

THE LOST JEWELS OF NABOOTI

CHOOSE FROM 38 ENDINGS!

BY R. A. MONTGOMERY

MYSTERY OF THE MAYA

CHOOSE
FROM 39
ENDINGS!

BY R. A. MONTGOMERY

HOUSE OF
DANGER

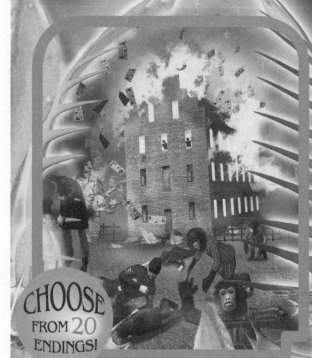

CHOOSE
FROM 20
ENDINGS!

BY R. A. MONTGOMERY

RACE FOREVER

CHOOSE FROM 33 ENDINGS!

BY R. A. MONTGOMERY

ESCAPE

CHOOSE
FROM 27
ENDINGS

BY R. A. MONTGOMERY

LOST ON THE AMAZON

CHOOSE FROM 28 ENDINGS!

BY R. A. MONTGOMERY

PRISONER OF THE ANT PEOPLE

CHOOSE FROM 28 ENDINGS!

BY R. A. MONTGOMERY

TROUBLE ON PLANET EARTH

CHOOSE FROM **22** ENDINGS!

BY R. A. MONTGOMERY

WAR WITH THE EVIL POWER MASTER

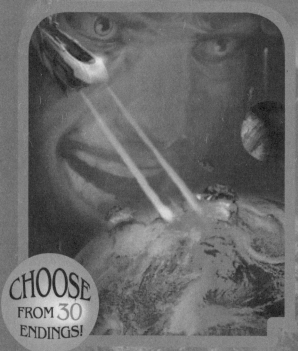

CHOOSE FROM 30 ENDINGS!

BY R. A. MONTGOMERY

CUP OF DEATH

CHOOSE FROM 23 ENDINGS!

BY SHANNON GILLIGAN

SECRET
OF THE NINJA

BY JAY LEIBOLD

THE BRILLIANT DR. WOGAN

CHOOSE FROM 20 ENDINGS!

BY R. A. MONTGOMERY

RETURN
TO ATLANTIS

CHOOSE
FROM **18**
ENDINGS!

BY R. A. MONTGOMERY

TERROR ON THE TITANIC

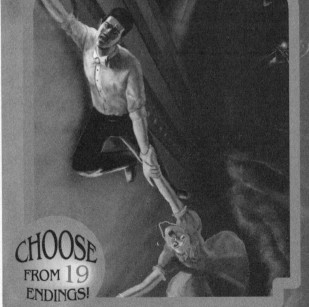

BY JIM WALLACE

TATTOO OF DEATH

This book is different from other books.

You and YOU ALONE are in charge of what happens in this story.

There are dangers, choices, adventures, and consequences. YOU must use all of your numerous talents and much of your enormous intelligence. The wrong decision could end in disaster—even death. But, don't despair. At anytime, YOU can go back and make another choice, alter the path of your story, and change its result.

Meeting new friends in martial arts class seemed innocent enough. But the next thing you know, you have a tattoo on your arm and belong to the Red Flowers, a gang involved in smuggling human cargo! You need to escape! But how? These people play for keeps. You had better practice your karate kick, because you are going to have to move fast to beat the most dangerous gang in town.

FORECAST FROM STONEHENGE

CHOOSE FROM 16 ENDINGS!

BY R. A. MONTGOMERY

INCA GOLD

CHOOSE FROM 16 ENDINGS!

BY JIM BECKET